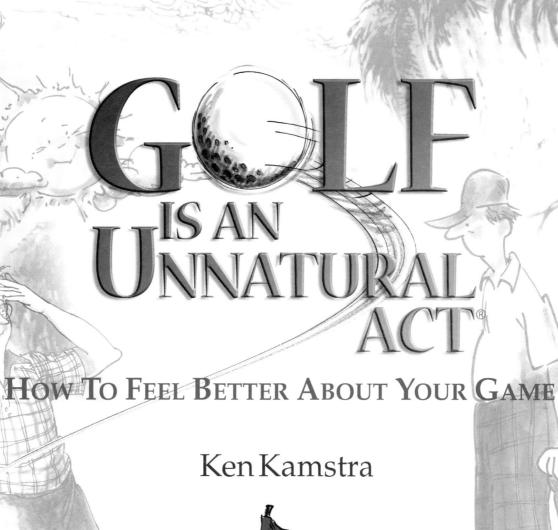

GOLF IS AN UNNATURAL ACT®

HOW TO FEEL BETTER ABOUT YOUR GAME

Ken Kamstra

Illustrations by Jack Lindstrom
Book design by Chris Long

THE IDEA SHELF

Original Edition
Published by The Idea Shelf, Inc., St.Paul, MN

Golf is an Unnatural Act
By Kenneth M. Kamstra

Published by :
The Idea Shelf, Inc.
Two Montcalm Hill
St. Paul, Minnesota 55116

Original Edition

Printed in the United States of America

This book is designed to provide information in regard
to the subject matter covered. Every effort has been
made to make it as complete and as accurate as possible.
However, there may be mistakes both typographical and
in content. The purpose of this book is to educate and
entertain. The author and The Idea Shelf, Inc. shall have
neither liability nor responsibility to any person or entity
with respect to any loss or damage caused, or alleged to
be caused, directly or indirectly by the information
contained in this book.

The terms "Pargoyle"and "Golf is an unnatural act"
are registered trademarks of Ken Kamstra.

Kamstra, Kenneth M.
    Golf is an unnatural act / by Kenneth M. Kamstra.
  -- 1st ed.
    p. cm.
    LCCN: 0-9671640-1-X
    ISBN: 2001 131930

Dedicated to
golfing under-achievers
everywhere

This book is for hackers. You know who you are. Reading this book will not improve your game but it can improve your attitude. Do you suspect paranoia when it seems that all the forces of nature are targeting you from the first moment you set foot on the golf course?

Do water hazards psyche you and swallow up your ball? Do trees block your every shot? Does that one perfect drive soar just over the hill and then disappear, never to be seen again? Why, when the sun is shining and the birds are singing, are you slowly going mad?

These occurrences are not paranoia; they are stark reality. There are evil forces – the dark side of nature – afoot to ruin your game, your day and even your life if you are a golfing addict. Why? Because "Golf is an unnatural act". Golf conflicts with the natural order of the universe.

The author's research into this chilling phenomenon goes back more than 500 years. An artist's rendition recreates that first golf swing. The one that loosed a supernatural curse over all the land. The curse of the "Pargoyles"! You cannot outwit them; you can learn to co-exist. Rejoice as you realize your score is beyond your control. It's not your fault.

Rejoice as you realize your score is beyond your control. It's not your fault.

From his home overlooking St.Paul, Minnesota, journalist/author Ken Kamstra ponders the plight of people obsessed by their hobbies and avocations. He "feels their pain" as well as their passions. His just-published book, "It's O.K. To Love Your Car" examines "Auto Erotic Dependency" (AED) and the worldwide car culture it has spawned. Millions happily endure this gene-induced car craze.

With this book, "Golf Is An Unnatural Act ", Kamstra applies his journalistic curiosity to an even larger addict population: golfers. His investigative research takes him back more than 500 years to the meadows of Scotland. Here, a lonely and bored shepherd is believed to have invented golf. This resourceful soul is also blamed for unwittingly unleashing a curse upon any citizen who would ever take up the game from that day forward and unto eternity.

The author counts himself among the world's worst hackers; so bad that even his best friends refuse to play with him. Still, he believes that you, like he, will feel better about your game when you know about the "Pargoyle's" Curse.

How golf came to be...

'TWAS 500 YEARS AGO. Some say longer.
Gargoyles atop a Scottish castle looked
down on a shepherd far below. Their
inscrutable smiles cast a benign approval
of the peaceful, pastoral scene.

Suddenly, a piercing yell shattered the
morning calm. Gargoyle grins turned
to scowls.

"I have invented golf!"
cried the shepherd.
And so he had.

Fashioning a credible driver from a tree limb, he drove a rounded rock from tree to tree, shouting joyfully with each hit. Soon all of Scotland took up the game; peasants and royalty alike. The once-bucolic countryside echoed with boisterous shouts, laughter, profanity. Windows were broken, trees battered, grass torn up.

Enraged at golfers' affront to the natural order of things, Gargoyles "morphed" themselves into Pargoyles; creatures reincarnated as trees, water, tall grass, sand. Their eternal mission: put a curse on all golfers; spoil their game; deny them the joy of making par.

In the dark of night on any golf course in the world, you can hear their blood-curdling cry ...

"Golf is an unnatural act!"

The PARGOYLES Curse

Water

Even a placid pond strikes terror in the
hearts of otherwise intrepid golfers.
Small wonder. Water is a natural hiding
place of dreaded Pargoyles.

THE Water Hazard

The sun is bright;
a day so glorious.
With par in reach,
I feel victorious.

Yet something lurks
I know he's there
Neath the water
in his lair.

And then I see it,
dark and steamy.
At water's edge,
I know he'll see me.

I stare into
the black abyss.
This crucial shot
I cannot miss.

With trembling hands,
I raise my four
and smash the ball,
then watch it soar.

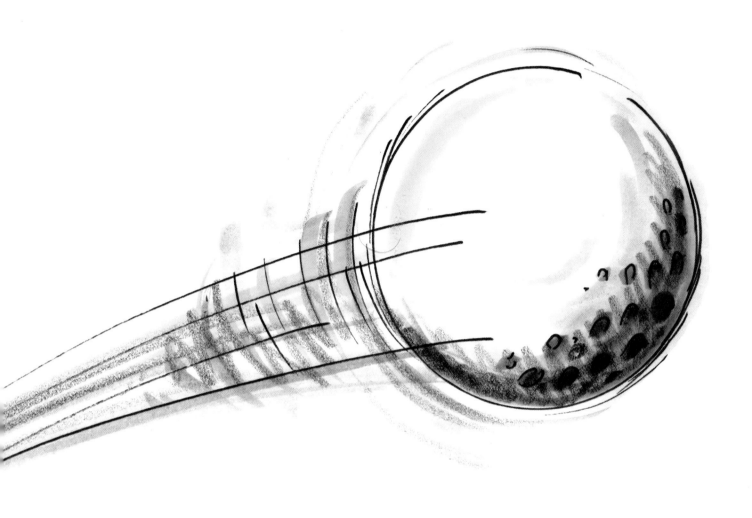

It arced on high
for just a second.
And then the creature
rose and beckoned.

My ball clutched tight,
he sank away.
Alas, I would not
par this day.

The ancient curse
was working still.
One cannot bend
a Pargoyle's will.

The PARGOYLES Curse

Sand

It's there to challenge your skills.
Test your temperament. Try your soul.
And maybe even worse.

The Fairway Bunker

*M*y instincts
did not warn at all.
My eyes, of course,
were on the ball.

Too late, I sensed
the Pargoyle's scheme.
I would not cry,
tho' I might scream.

How could I know
this ground was hallowed?
It's so unfair
that I be swallowed.

My wedge I clutched.
I know not why.
The golfers' code
demands I try.

The sun goes down
and I am beaten.
I wonder if
my kids have eaten.

Somewhere there
are golfers playing.
For me, I'll turn
to serious praying.

The PARGOYLES Curse

Separation

Beware of leaving your foursome
to track an errant ball.
Something may be tracking you.

THE Out of Bounder

Hope, not wisdom
made me follow,
when "out-of-bounds"
my ball did swallow.

A penalty stroke
I could have taken.
Now I'm lost
and feel forsaken.

My friends will fret,
"that big, dumb lug",
then they'll play on
with just a shrug.

We share, of course,
this golf addiction.
If I survive,
there'll be no friction.

I hear a crunching
sound behind.
The Pargoyle curse
creeps in my mind.

I'd sell my soul
if he would free me.
My pals I know
would love to see me.

The PARGOYLES

The

Curse

Vanishment

Why does your golf ball
sometimes vanish in play?
There is an answer,
but you are better off not knowing.

THE **B**all
Mole

A mighty "thwack";
the ball soared high.
Straight and true,
an easy lie.

I saw it fall
just o'er the mound.
No hunt and search
this time around.

With happy heart,
I viewed the pin.
A stroke or two
and I'd be in.

But then the worst
I could have feared.
That ball of mine
had disappeared.

On hands and knees
in disbelief;
where could he hide,
this golfball thief?

A munching sound,
I thought I heard.
The "Ball Mole" dining
That's too absurd.

The PARGOYLES Curse

Lessons

Your body was never meant
to contort itself this way.
"It's unnatural", you whine to your instructor.
The Pargoyle's smile is all-knowing.

The Instructor

You raise your club
but friends just snicker.
A pro might help
your drive look slicker.

'Twas golf's cruel lure
caused your seduction.
Be warned you'll need
intense instruction.

Lock those fingers
round the shaft!
The trainer's scorn
shows through his laugh.

This grotesque way
my limbs are bent;
it cannot be
the Lord's intent.

The pro's loud screams
awake suspicion.
Is this a Pargoyle
on a mission?

With painful limbs
and spirits broken,
a graduate now
or Pargoyle token?

We'll live our lives
with golfer's strife;
neglecting work
and family life.

Unnatural is this
so called game.
One must keep trying
just the same.

The

PARGOYLES

Curse

The Green

Vulnerable victims,
women are the target-of-choice
for Pargoyle mischief. Lady beware.
Putt alone and you
put yourself at serious risk.

The Downhill Putt

I'm on the green
in only two.
If not a birdie,
par will do.

They say our boobs
get in the way.
I care not what
old geezers say.

It scares me though
when tales they utter;
how Pargoyles snare
a hapless putter.

I stroke the ball
as taught to do;
but is the green
in motion too?

The ball won't sink
but now my heart does.
A paw appears
where once my ball was

'Tis my right
to play this game.
I'll switch to tennis
just the same.

The

PARGOYLES

Curse

The Rough

Follow your ball into the rough.
You learn humility there.
You curse your rotten luck.
But are you cursed too?

THE Rough

I've hooked before
and sliced a few.
The rough to me
is nothing new.

But now there is
this sense of dread.
An eye appears
and then a head.

The Pargoyle curse
transcends the ages.
So they warned,
those clubhouse sages.

I try to run;
the grass holds tight.
The monster's tail
blocks any flight.

Should I survive
and make it out,
the Pargoyle's curse
I'll never doubt.

At the bar, I'll
join their laughter.
They'll ne'r believe

...I've seen hereafter.

The

PARGOYLES

Curse

Trees

Behold the magnificent, mighty oak.
One of nature's crowning achievements.
Confront the majestic tree
with your puny club and you
risk the wrath of the Pargoyle Curse.

The Mighty Oak

The mighty oak,
it has me cowering
with arms outstretched
and face that's glowering.

"You shall not pass!"
it snarls at me.
How can it speak?
It's just a tree.

A tree whose gnarled
arms do stretch
to block each shot
of this poor wretch.

My foursome waits.
They'll think I joke.
You've been in battle
with an oak?

Me thinks I hear
fierce Gaelic growls
from deep inside
the old oak's bowels.

The Pargoyle curse
lives on in trees;
doth bring this duffer
to his knees.

It's not your fault